Backwards into the Future

Backwards into the Future
Chaos in the Classroom

Arnold De Graaff

Heathwood Press
Holt

Backwards into the Future
Chaos in the Classroom

First Edition

For information, contact Heathwood Press
www.heathwoodpress.com

Printed in the United Kingdom.
Published in the United Kingdom by Heathwood Press,
Trade Name of Robert Smith, Holt, United Kingdom.

Edited by R.C. Smith
Cover design by Beth Titchiner
ISBN 978-0-9570961-1-0

Table of Contents

Forward by R.C. Smith

For the reader who is concerned with the increasing distortion of our children's education, the failed and ultimately regressive political policy as well as the permeation and pervasion of capitalist ideology which has lead to that distortion, this book will be found richly rewarding.

To its credit, *Backwards into the Future* is not an overly academic work. Today, at a time when academic practice is subject to extreme abstraction and in some cases almost entirely disconnected from the concrete phenomena of life and experience, this book balances wonderfully between coherent academic critique and the voice of practical conversation. It was originally written as a public presentation and for that, the work itself is not subject to the academic divide but rather to the type of voice that unites a community under the insight of practical critique. From a man and a writer who has devoted a significant part of his life to understanding the problems of education, Arnold De Graaff shows the wonderful and often deprived character of what it means to speak, firstly, as a concerned citizen. At the same time his sensitivity allows him to emphasize the urgency of the hour and of the practical actions and efforts that we must collectively put forth, if we are to strive not to meet the decay of our children's education with ideological blindness and pacification. Consequently, the meeting in which this public presentation arises takes a more humane form – that of an exchange of views – and highlights the many critical realities that concern the community in the hope that as a community, we might finally refuse to accept the ideological practice which has claimed the very vision of our childrens' futures.

But let me insist that owing to the force of circumstances, namely of the global capitalist vision of life and the extreme distortions and absurdity subject to that totalized worldview, this work does not shy away from the harsh reality of our society. In his hope to bring together the immediate community, De Graaff does not resort to a misguided state of politics or to an abstract philosophy as a frame of reference. He offers the opportunity to first look inside of ourselves, individually and collectively, to what simply speaks as being the right thing to do. The author presents a case that sensitively evokes both the community's suffering in the midst of the destructiveness of the global capitalist totality and the spreading fires of corporatization and commercialization, as well as our common passion anchored in the the multicoloured and multidimensional phenomena of our experience. De Graaff illustrates in such a grounded way the needless suffering that our children face in a future that is becoming increasingly closed to them, and lays out some of the basic distortions of experience that contribute to this ultimately regressive path whilst also capturing the greater economic unbalance that grows by the day.

On the technical side of things, the direction of thought that De Graaff offers is foundational and much needed. His call for not only an educational curriculum that opens the child up to the multidimensional coherence of experience, but also one that affirms and promotes healthy self-development and intimate and open engagement with phenomena. These are fundamental arguments that we are just starting to apprehend more philosophically (in terms of alternative epistemology, anthropology and cosmology). On the same token, the idea that the child (or individual adult for that matter) is a free flourishing subject, and that a progressive or coherent curriculum is one that promotes concrete autonomy in connection with an understanding of the phenomenal world of experience as dynamic, intersubjecctive, multidimensional and certainly particular before general, is tantamount to the type of foundational perspective that radical educational discourse is presently lacking.

This book, I feel, is one that has much to offer when it comes to understanding both the dilemmas that we face in education today, and the ways in which we may consider moving toward a more just and humane approach to our childrens' growth and development.

R. C. Smith

Publisher's Note

Heathwood has done its utmost to preserve the rawness of this work in its original format as a public presentation. A number of diagrams and tables were presented to the audience during the original speech, some of which we have included at the end of each chapter for the reader's interest.

Introduction

You may be wondering why I am doing a presentation on education. The answer is very simple. Like many of you, I have two grandchildren in school and two more to come, as well as two little nieces. Secondly, along with many doctors, artists, craftsmen, businessmen, social workers, shop keepers, counsellors and professionals - anyone who has children in the education system today - we all find ourselves in a position of concern when it comes to our children's learning and development. Thirdly, I have been curious about what is really happening in education for a while now. In fact, I used to be quite involved in education and three months ago a review by Michelle Landsberg turned me on to Alfie Kohn's book *The Schools Our Children Deserve*. Since then I have tried to get as up to date as I can on the current problems of education. That doesn't make me an expert. What I am presenting tonight is a combination of my previous experience in education and what I've been able to gather in the last three months. I have read many articles and books; checked sources; found an amazing number of resources; and generally became both very disturbed about the new funding, curriculum, report cards and tests as well as very excited about the new, alternative possibilities. My main emphasis will be on the curriculum: the new program of studies introduced by the government and on what an alternative curriculum could look like.

Here is the outline (see Table 1). I wish I could skip the large middle section on the role of the government, the consequences of its policies and the corporate vision of life. Since many others are analyzing these parts I will be as brief as possible and summarize that part so we can end by looking at alternative programs and possibilities.

Table 1

Outline for Speech on Education: "Backwards into the Future: Chaos in the Classroom"				
What Parents want for their children	The new Ontario curriculum —— An integrated curriculum	-The debate within education -The changes the government has introduced -The corporate agenda -The corporate vision of life -The effects on our schools	Renewal in the last 30 years ⟶ Examples of integrated programs and schools	What we can do

Before I jump right in with the new Kindergarten curriculum, let's stop and take an opinion poll.

How would you like your children or the youth of our town to turn out?

What are your long-term goals for them?

What do you want your children to be taught about life?

Please jot your responses down on a piece of paper. In a moment we will compare notes. We will keep these different reactions, hopes and wishes before us. And we will come back to them toward the end of the evening. At this point I'd like to read you a letter from two concerned parents. I trust that it will become clear as we go along why they are taking the stance they do. You may not agree, but I hope that their decision will make sense to you.

Dear teacher and principal:

As you notice, I am not addressing you by your name since this letter is not to you personally. I am assuming that you are as distressed about the direction our schools are going as I am. You must be in a terrible bind. Although I appreciate what you are doing with my children and the school, there are some very basic things that need to change. And my husband and I want to do our part to make that happen. We have given this a lot of thought. We have carefully read the curriculum guides and some recent books about education. We have looked at some of the best evidence and research available about what makes for good learning and teaching and what discourages learning.

We have come to the conclusion that we can no longer allow our children to do their usual homework of filling in worksheets and workbooks as well as projects that don't have a meaningful context that our children understand. The best research has concluded that there is no measurable benefit from the usual skill and drill kind of homework kids do. It does not improve their performance in any way, neither in elementary or secondary school.

Instead of their homework we will spend half an hour to an hour each day reading (books of their choice) and responding to their reading in different ways (see their "story envelopes" for responses and activities), or playing games that include number concepts and developing an art portfolio for the year. We are also looking into some interesting and meaningful projects from other schools on the Internet that we might join or do ourselves.

Secondly, we will not allow our oldest son in grade three to participate in the province-wide language arts and math testing this upcoming spring. For those three days we are planning some special outings to the Young People's Theatre, and the Museum. We have come to the conclusion – after reading the overwhelming evidence – that this kind of testing is very detrimental to learning, and that generally, it affects the atmosphere and teaching in the school (teaching to the test). We gather the tests are quite flawed and that they mostly measure basic skills and isolated concepts but not any real understanding and comprehension. Standardized testing encourages individualism and competition with personal success and a well-paying job as the primary goal for his life. Besides that being a bit of a hoax, we don't want that carrot dangling in front of him; nor do we want to condition our son to mindlessly jump through whatever hoops it takes to get to the top or give up and become discouraged and lose interest in learning. We want something different for our children. We think that there are higher goals for life and many other values that we treasure. We will inform the Ministry of Education and Training and the Board of Trustees of our decision as well.

Finally, we do not want an evaluation attached to every piece of work our children bring home from school. Schools are not for tests and constant evaluation. Moreover, we do not want the new reports cards for our children sent home. We believe that they are detrimental and also quite meaningless. A teacher interview will suffice for us. We will encourage our sons to bring their "story envelopes" and their "art portfolios" and have them tell you what they have learned and enjoyed. Maybe they can do the same with their class work.

We are sending a letter to the local newspapers asking them to refuse to publish the test scores and if they feel they have to publish them we have asked them to print the scores in the sports section, which seems most fitting.

We are also getting together with some other parents to share what we have learned and to see what joint action we can take. We want to help each other, especially those parents who work shifts, come home late or don't have the resources to help their children with their education at home. We were encouraged to learn that other parents in Colorado, Ohio and Michigan are boycotting standardized testing.

Meanwhile, for the time being at least, I am resigning from the School Council. I don't want to do fundraising for programs and textbooks that I don't agree with; nor do I care to continue to talk about inconsequential matters. Right now I'd rather spend my time finding good learning resources for our children.

Sincerely yours,
(A Parent)

1

The New Ontario Curriculum 1-8 and Kindergarten Program

Let's start our critique of the new curriculum with the Kindergarten Program, because it sets the stage for all the other grades from one through eight. We could call this program: "From the Sublime to the Ridiculous." It starts out wonderful and raises high expectations that this is going to be about genuine reform.

The introduction to the curriculum reflects decades of careful observation and study of how five year olds develop, think and learn and how best to encourage them in this kind of learning. Here is a summary:

- This Kindergarten Program encourages integrated and interconnected learning which focuses on real-life situations and activities that are relevant to their lives. Moreover, the learning activities must build on and connect with the children's past experiences.

- Such an integrated program will address all the dimensions of the child's experience and interrelate the intellectual, physical, social, emotional and creative dimensions; it will develop the children's abilities in a wide range of areas.

- It will encourage self-expression and self-discovery through music, drama and rich language activities; it will allow the child to express feelings of wonder and curiosity about the world, and talk about their own interest and preferences, express their own thoughts and share their experiences.

- In this program the uniqueness of each child will be honoured and the curriculum will take into account that children are at different developmental levels and learn at different times and in different ways. Moreover, it will take into account that children come from diverse backgrounds and languages and may take time to adjust to a new situation. In view of these differences flexible learning and teaching approaches must be used, ones that recognize personal strengths and accomplishments.

- The curriculum will provide opportunities to explore, create, question, attempt, experiment, reflect, all of which will develop creative and critical thinking, problem solving, reasoning and inquiry skills.

- All of this will be done through hands-on experiences and concrete materials and activities, and especially through play. It involves learning by doing – the best kind of learning, including math through everyday activities.

- Such a program of learning will develop positive attitudes to learning – if not a love of learning. The curriculum will develop self-reliance and confidence; children will attempt new tasks and show independence. The program will involve cooperative activities with peers and will foster consideration for others.

- And finally all of this will happen in a safe, secure, inviting, pleasant, non-threatening atmosphere in which children can identify and share their feelings and emotions. The children will be able to communicate their needs, develop positive attitudes toward themselves and others. In this context they will be encouraged to listen and respond to each other and develop their social skills.

- Assessment of the children's development and learning will be done in the context of everyday classroom activities and through observation.

Wow! What a curriculum. So far so good - one can hardly identify anything backwards about this. On first look, the new curriculum behind the Kindergarten Program seems very positive. Even if your child has some difficulties, he or she is in safe hands; and what a program for a multicultural class of kids, or for an inner city school with many kids from various backgrounds; and what a treat it must be for Kindergarten teachers to be able to teach in schools with these kind of mandates! On this read of the new curriculum, it also speaks eloquently for the Ontario public school system of the last thirty years; its slow but steady progress through some trial and error, but nevertheless pushing forward. I want to come back to this later on to unmask one of the many myths about public education. Meanwhile, we can hang on to this affirmative emphasis on the Kindergarten Program as a basis for further development and genuine change.

But first we must look at the ridiculous, the mundane, the trivial, the deceptive, and ultimately the destructive part of this new curriculum. Unfortunately, it is the part that dominates grades one through eight and the secondary school program, which cancels out all of the goods aspects that we have just identified in the Kindergarten Program. After the mostly positive introduction, one would think that there would be an outline of exciting, rich, integrated, real-life kinds of units and themes. Units on plants or animals, on water or weather, on the neighbourhood or transportation, or even a unit on machines; all of the things in a five year olds' particular surroundings and experience. Maybe even a unit on the body and sensory awareness or on becoming aware of others and building trust; and throughout exposure to children's literature, developing puppet plays, and so on – that is, a rich, full program which touches all of the aspects of the child's being. Instead what we get is lists of expectations – to be exact: one-hundred and twenty-four of them – many of which deal with fragmented, isolated, out of context, abstracted little concepts and skills.

Allow me to give you a few examples of this:

- The child must demonstrate awareness of some conventions of written materials (e.g., text is written from left to right; words have spaces between them; words are spelled with upper and lower case letters).

Almost all children that have any exposure to words – whether from being read to; by watching the television; writing their own name – already know intuitively that words go from left to right and have spaces between them, and the basic difference between capitals and small letters – unless, of course, they are from another culture. How trivial and silly can we be, now that our teachers are supposed to assess and report on each of these kind of expectations.

Another example from the subject of Writing:

-The child must write using a variety of tools and media (e.g., crayons, paper, computer, chalkboard, coloured markers, cardboard).

Imagine your child's teacher having to report that your son or daughter has done well using coloured markers but has failed or refused to use crayons; and that he or she is still quite hesitant about writing on the chalkboard but enjoys cardboard. The curriculum is full of these kinds of self-evident, ridiculous and trivial expectations both on the kindergarten level and throughout grades one through eight. I haven't counted how many of the more than four-thousand expectations from kindergarten through grade eight are of this nature, but there are many. So much for this rigorous, new curriculum with its high standards. A more appropriate word would be "substandard". As one parent said, "there is a lot of fluff in this curriculum." But there is more, and now we can turn our focus to a much more serious part of our discussion.

A second group of expectations has to do with the fragmented, isolated, out of context, abstracted concepts and skills that must be taught, assessed, tested for and reported on. Basically, the authors of the new curriculum have taken the scientific concepts and vocabulary of the academic disciplines like mathematics, physics, technology, biology, chemistry, physiology, geography, social sciences, music theory, etc. and broken them down to small segments and, in turn, have tried to find a concrete example to illustrate the concept. You could call this: the backward curriculum.

Instead of requiring basic understanding and knowledge of real-life situations (i.e., plants, animals, things, relations, events and so on), what is required is the teaching of abstract concepts and skills. Most of these expectations dealing with fragmented little scientific concepts and skills start with "identity", "classify", "describe", or "name". Rather than being directed toward concrete reality in its wholeness, the way kids and all of us experience life, our children are taught to encounter abstract concepts floating around in the universe.

Let me give you a few examples from the area of Science and Technology, both of which are from the Kindergarten and Grade two curriculum guides:

- The child must "describe some differences between living and non-living things (kindergarten)."
- The child must "identify and describe the physical characteristics of different types of animals."
- The child must "classify a variety of animals."
- The child must "identify and describe behavioural characteristics that enable animals to survive (grade two)."

Nowhere is there any expectation to come to know the rich and wonderful animal world as a whole and in its concreteness. In fact, it isn't until grade six that students get the opportunity to study the animal world as a whole. But even then the child only gets to study the classification system – an abstract biological concept dealing with how animals are categorized. It is a difference between "this dog, my pet" and "all dogs have these characteristics." Bad or what we call distorted Science goes from the specific or the particular – this particular animal – to the general – all animals, and therefore suppresses the particularity of each phenomenon. That has to do with the distortion of our logical (or experiential) distinguishing, with establishing the identity of things (this is a tree, that is not). A and non-A. It has to do with general laws that hold for all animals or groups of animals, with general concepts which therefore subsume the particulars of our experience.

So what is so bad about children learning the scientific concepts, skills and vocabulary of the various disciplines? Well, that depends. It depends on what you like your child to know about animals and more generally what you would like him or her to know at the time of their graduation.

Let me draw out the differences between the two kinds of knowledge a little more and how they could be integrated more meaningfully.

Table 2

The Kindergarten Program

Language	Mathematics	Science and Technology	Personal and Social Development	The Arts
-Oral Communication	-Number Sense and Numeration	-Exploration and Experimentation	-Self-Awareness and Self-Reliance	-Creative Activity
-Reading	-Measurement	-Use of Technology	-Health and Physical Activity	-Response to Art Works
-Writing	-Spatial Sense and Geometry		-Social Relationships	-Knowledge of Elements and Forms
-Understanding of Media Materials	-Patterning		-Awareness of Surroundings	
	-Data Measurement and Probability			

Table 3

An Integrated Perspective (Overview of Grades K, 1-3)			
The Earth	Plants	Animals	People
- The Earth in Space - Weather - Seasons - Air - Water - Land & Soils - Physical Things - Energy -Forces & Movement	- Exploring the Plant World -What Plants Need to Grow - Growing Plants for Food and Clothing -Trees and Forestry -Conservation	- Exploring the Animal World - Enjoying and Caring for Animals -People Raising & Using Animals -Wildlife Reserves -Endangered Species	- You are Special: (Senses, Feelings, Growth; Diet) -Families -Friends -Where People Live -Working Together -Providing for Everyone's Needs -Fairness for Everybody (Urban, Rural Communities) (Pioneer Life)
	Interrelationships		

2

An Alternative Approach: An Integrated Program

Describing "some differences between living and non-living things" could be all right if it were a part of a larger, more meaningful whole. For then it would be a part of helping 5 year olds develop a beginning frame of reference: of making sense out of the world; of providing an overview and an orientation. Developmentally it would help the child to move from fantasy and imagination and magical thinking to more concrete and reality-oriented thinking.

Then they would first have to be introduced, for example, to different "things" in the world; to the realm of earth, the land; to the realm of plants, of animals; and of people living and working together and the interconnectedness between all areas of life. They would have to collect pictures, make charts, etc. of the different realms. And in that context it would be meaningful to ask: "How can you tell if something belongs to one realm or another? How do you know whether something is living or non-living? What do plants need to live? Do rocks need the same things? How are people different from plants and animals? How do they all depend on and need each other? And after this kind of discussion – and only after this kind of discussion, if the whole exercise is to stay meaningful – and after some integrating activities like making a collage, or a painting, or a class mural to which every child contributes, or reading different poems from different cultures, etc. After that, it makes sense to introduce the animal world, whether Kindergarten, grade one or two. For now there is somewhere to place it. There is a frame of reference, however rudimentary, which begins from being grounded in life.

Dealing with the animal world, again the children would need some kind of introduction, some view of the whole: the place of animals in the whole of life. They can be helped to see that animals are an essential part of life; see the different ways we depend on them; how they enrich our lives; how we ought to care for animals; and so on. A part of our calling with regard to life is:

to care for, to protect – not to misuse and exploit animals. After some general activities, like observing and discussing what animals are like; making a chart or a display; enjoying a film or a story; etc., they are ready to explore the animal world in some detail. And at this age (ages five, six, seven) children need to experience animals as concretely as possible (pets, farm animals, pond animals, fish, etc.) and be allowed to respond to them in many different ways. They need to be helped to broaden and deepen their understanding through observing, writing, discovering, constructing, via research, films, stories, poems, music, art, and dance. Each child ought to be able to choose his or her own ways of responding and be encouraged to explore other avenues. For each type of response is as valid and valuable as any other response. Because animals are more than their scientific name and characteristics; they are more than their experiential identity. As living creatures, as phenomena, they are multidimensional subjects. They function in all aspects of life. And the biological way of coming to know animals (their experiential identity) is not more valid than the aesthetic way or any other way. Children experience animals in a more total way: the beauty of animals; they way in which they move; the vital role they play in each child's life (food, clothing and many other things); the deep feelings they develop towards animals (love, fear, hate); caring for them as pets; imitating their sounds and movements; coming to know how people have worshipped animals or revere the spirit of the animal; or how animals are portrayed in art and music.

Through such experiences and sharing them with each other, children are helped to broaden and deepen their view of life.

At this point some of you may still wonder, "but what about the facts? Isn't this all too fluffy and child-oriented? isn't it more effective to give them facts and test them on it?" An understandable response because that is how many of us were taught. But think again. It all depends what kind of knowledge, attitudes and values you would like your children to acquire, in this case toward animals.

Table 4

The Many Integral Ways Children Come to Know (through many-sided involvement and responses)

By...	
- Relating and sharing experiences	Animals
	Weather
	Water
- Discussing	Plants
	Air
- Listening	Neighbourhood
	Transportation
- Observing and viewing	Energy
	Tools
- Researching	Machines
	Land
- Constructing	Space
	Themselves
- Creative writing	Each Other
	Their Bodies
- Singing songs	Ponds
	Wetlands
- Movement and dance	Streams
	Towns
- Reading stories and poems	Maps
	Forests
- Report writing	Farms
	Fire Fighters
- Making a display	Butterflies
	Birds
- Dramatizing	Stars
	Clouds
- Making a graph & working with numbers	Fears
	Happiness
- Sharing activities and projects	Friends
	Family

Table 5

Different Kinds of Knowledge

Integral, experiential, contextual, particular, personal knowledge	Scientific, analytic, knowledge
Ultimate knowledge (Values; vision of life; life, death, birth, history, meaning, wisdom) **Relational knowledge** (love, commitment, relationships, friendships)	-Verifying -Evaluating
"Sense of justice & fairness" knowledge	-Defining
Social knowledge (interrelatedness, roles, dignity) **"Communication skill" knowledge** (clarity, expressiveness)	-Communicating -Summarizing -Reasoning
Skills knowledge (doing, making, constructing) **Perception, "distinguishing" knowledge** **Symbolic knowledge** **Sensitivity knowledge** **Bodily knowledge** **Energetic knowledge** **Movement knowledge**	-Experimenting -Predicting -Hypothesizing -Conceptualizing -Gathering Data -Observing

Table 6

<u>Intelligences</u>

Interpersonal Intelligence

Linguistic Intelligence

Logical-Mathematical Intelligence

Musical Intelligence

Intrapersonal Intelligence

Bodily-Kinaesthetic

Spatial Intelligence

H. Gardner, 1991

3

_____

Different Kinds of Knowledge

There is a lot of writing and agreement today that as people we all want to make sense out of our world and our own lives. We need to feel orientated and to have a sense of identity. We may be instinctual creatures, or rational animals or political animals, and so on; but above all, ultimately, we are existentially inclined to discern some meaning in the world. And I take that in the full sense of the word – total meaning and not just cognitive or analytical meaning, rational or political. A person may not have much formal education yet have a lot of knowledge about life, about relations, about fairness; about her work; about her horses. A very rich kind of knowledge, experiential knowledge. An integrated curriculum dealing with concrete life situations can help children develop such basic meanings, a grounded frame of reference or a concrete vision of life. And that is how they find their identity and their place and calling in response to the evocativeness of life as well as the concrete phenomena of their situations. Such perspectival and integrative knowledge involves responsibility and care. Because particular, experiential knowledge of something makes us responsible. It is simply recognizing the fact that every experience we have is in interaction with some particular thing, some particular phenomenon. We can either turn our backs against the concrete stuff of our experiences, which speak and are given to us, or we can remain sensitively aware of them. These trees here in Monora Park or on this playground, ought to be cared for, preserved, developed and maintained and not carelessly or unnecessarily destroyed. Or, I ought to make sure that my horse and cows in this pasture have enough water and do not starve to death.

    This kind of knowledge is quite different from overly conceptual knowledge. It is grounded firstly in our interacting with the particular phenomenon; secondly, in our gaining a general sense of orientation with it. It is the difference between "this tree" or "this animal" that I have come to know about and "all trees need air, water and food." One is particular, the other is general. Experientially grounded knowledge can and does incorporate more general awareness of something as another way to deepen our understanding of these particular animals. The more I know generally about animals, the more it helps me to take care of *this* animal – that is my responsibility. It too can help us to do – what I call – the truth as it is *given* to us with regard to animals or trees or whatever else. This kind of curriculum not only provides a frame of reference, but it also provides a meaningful context for skill development. There are many wonderful examples of such integrated skill building in the context of exciting and challenging units. Either intuitively or by design, many teachers teach in this holistic way – or used to...

What we get instead in this new curriculum is the promotion of overly conceptual, abstract type of knowledge. We get fragmented, little concepts and skills devoid of much meaning and largely unrelated to the particulars of the child's world and experience. It is a reductionistic view of knowledge: a type of abstract, overly conceptual knowledge without experiential context or grounding. I call it a peripheral curriculum.

The curious thing about the Kindergarten curriculum is that it is left up to the teacher to choose the themes, units and activities "that emphasize the integrated nature of learning through which the learning expectations can be achieved." Although on another page it states that the Board (of Education) must decide how expectations can best be achieved within the total Kindergarten program.

All this means is that there is a big hole in the middle of the curriculum. There is no meaningful content and that is true for much of the material of all the grades. In the middle of the curriculum universe there is a black hole. Around this black hole, however, are hundreds of learning expectations – the little fragmented abstract concepts and skills. Well, perhaps that *is* the curriculum - maybe that is the only content?

The answer is "yes", that is the curriculum. The hundreds of silly, abstracted, isolated and sometimes developmentally dubious concepts and skills – if taken seriously – make the development of any meaningful themes and units impossible or seem contradictory. There is no time to *teach*, assess and test for these concepts and skills. To do that well takes a lot of time. Since there is no time, teachers have to resort to workbooks and worksheets. Any sensitivity to the child's feelings, experiences, way of learning, life-situation, etc. is undercut by the constant evolution, testing, and reporting on fragmented facts and sub-skills. There is no time for developing any meaningful content with children; to engage them in genuine learning and to assess their real progress. In fact, under one Board teachers are told to start with the expectation, then look at the assessment, and then figure out what kind of lesson is needed. That is properly called "teaching to the test." Never mind meaning, context, interest, involvement or concrete life situation. Meanwhile I haven't even mentioned – besides the silly things and abstracted concepts of this curriculum – the developmentally inappropriate concepts.

This kind of curriculum lays the foundation for a one-dimensional view of life and experience with an emphasis on overly conceptual (identitarian) thinking and distorted technological know-how. But this should not be mistake as a crusade against science or technology. Rather, it is a rally against science and technology separated from a meaningful, experiential context. It is an argument against fragmentation and dividing the world into disciplines. It is arguing for integration and opening reality up to the student in all its richness. This view is therefore against scientism, which is properly understood as the distortion of science and the functionalizing of a one-dimensional view of reality. "In science is our trust and technology leads the way." Instead what I am arguing for is for a holistic view of life in which all dimensions of life equally have their rightful place.

It would seem that the main emphasis of the new curriculum is to develop ungenuine little scientists, technicians and logicians out of children that can use distorted scientific vocabulary correctly and who have mastered abstracted, fragmented concepts and skills – at least for the duration of the test, stored in their short-term memory. Even this stated emphasis however has no basis in reality. To do all the little experiments and investigations requires a lot of time and resources. But there is little funding for the equipment needed. With regard to funding the government simply says: "look elsewhere, to the private sector, or do your own fundraising." And in order to cover all the required concepts and skills, there is no time for so called 'higher-order' thinking: problem solving, hypothesizing, experimenting, gathering data, drawing conclusions, etc. So teachers in fact are reduced to teach and test for the little, abstract concepts and skills regardless of whether or not it is meaningful, or whether or not the child understands it. As one mother told me: her son "did a great job on his project, with our help, but he didn't have a clue what it meant or why he was doing it." That is because this new curriculum ultimately leads to a de-skilling of teachers. After a few years of this approach, we may only need teacher assistants or technicians. Meanwhile we can only feel sorry for the hundreds of students flocking to teachers' colleges. Little do they know what they are actually in for. But let us stop here for a moment to get a broader perspective of the debate within education.

4

The Basic Debate in Education

There is indeed an intense struggle going on between two radically different points of view. And the debate gets extremely heated at times with accusations flying back and forth. Although this battle is going on within the educational arena, the conflict is not really about education itself. And that is what makes this argument so frustrating and maddening. If the conflict was really about the need for the continual renewal of our educational system, we could sit down together, look at the evidence, and check decades of research and teachers' experience. Then, slowly, we would be able to come to a consensus and map out a common direction. The grandiose "Reform" introduced by our government has very little to do with improving our schools, raising standards, ensuring greater accountability and more parent involvement. That is the propaganda, but not the reality. If it were, the government would have presented a very different picture of the state of public education and of what would be needed for further development. It would have appealed to very different evidence based on decades of research and practice. Instead it has taken recourse to creating a crisis mentality, and has put its weight behind one side of the argument not because of concern about our public school system, but to implement its own political and economic agenda, as we will see a little later.

Nevertheless, since a lot of the battle is happening within the educational arena, we need to be up-to-date on that conflict. Besides clarifying the issues it will also help us to find a clear, solid and secure direction for educational renewal and what we can do about it.

The rest of the battle needs to be fought on the broader political and ideological level. Many are already at work trying to create change on that level and we can join them.

However, we need not wait for that battle to be settled politically and economically. We can act meaningfully now – in our schools here, locally, and help implement a different kind of learning for our children. Here too, we are not alone. There are many quiet, unobtrusive renewals going on in classrooms all over Canada, the United States and the world, in spite of government reforms and regulations.

As one educator suggested to me: "We need to put this curriculum on the shelf as a sort of reference about minimal standards for education and then go on with the real business of renewing and developing our educational system."

So what is this underlying conflict going on in education? One simple and quick way to look at this complex issue is to look at the following diagram.[1] It presents two historically and culturally opposing ideals for society and its institutions, including education: the distorted, abstractly conceptual Ideal argued in the name of scientism, and the Freedom Ideal.

In the one, nature, including human nature must be controlled and conditioned by means of scientism and technicism. It is the equivalent to an unduly abstracted, reified, no longer experientially grounded ideal, which is tantamount to reducing things to their logical dimension, separating them from their rich coherence with all the other dimensions, so that the word "bird", for example, becomes just a (abstracted, separated, isolated) concept and not a general word for a wonderful and complex reality. In this view the child is easily seen as raw material that must be shaped or conditioned. In this view the child is easily demonized and must be controlled. In the other view the person must be free to realize his or her own inner potential – the self-realization of the human personality. Such a view can easily lead to an idealized or romantic view of the child. These two opposing ideals can be seen in the writing's of B.F. Skinner's *Walden Two* (1948) and A.S. Neill's *Summerhill* (1960). As is often true of extreme opposites, historically it soon gave rise to a third position that combines the "truth" of both. A good example of this "in-between-position" is the *English Infant Schools* (1971). You could call this view "Freedom within Structure." In the British infant schools (ages four to either six or nine), for example, the maths corner would be carefully structured in terms of difficulty and variety, covering all the levels and concepts. Yet the child is free

---

[1] Please see Table 7 at the end of this chapter.

to take up any of the activities and problems it chooses. The teacher keeps careful track of what the child covers and challenges her or him to explore some new areas.

Today the rhetoric can have touches of the same extreme opposites. The Back-to-Basics on the one side and Progressive Education on the other side. But here too, over the decades a carefully worked out and researched third alternative has emerged. I call it: *"The Child as a Free Flourishing Subject."* We might also call it *"The Child as Initiator of His or Her own Learning"* or *"The Child as Autonomous and Efficacious"*. It is characterized by student choice, active discovery, challenging tasks and projects, careful evaluation, cooperative learning and skill development within the context of meaning and above all, an integrated curriculum that helps the child to make sense of the world. Moreover, this third alternative might also be characterized in light of the child as active on his or her own behalf and bearing responsibility, as therefore actively engaged in his or her own learning. Most importantly this approach emphasises on the very basic fact that the child should be able to develop his or her own frame of reference and orientation in the world and as he or she searches and look for meaning. It requires very active involvement of the teacher and very active learning on the part of the student. We could call it experientially grounded forming that leads to self-forming or experientially grounded guiding that leads to self-guidance. The idea of the "child as an efficacious agent" emphasizes that it is not enough for the teacher to engage in "direct teaching" but that the child must make it her own – incorporate it in her own frame of reference and expand her understanding of the world. This means that the child should be in charge of his or her own learning with the guidance of a teacher. If we are not merely to condition the child, or worse, to brainwash and violate the child's sense of self – the child as active on her own behalf and bearing responsibility – then we need to ensure that the child is actively engaged in learning and open to ever-unfolding self-discovery.

Historically and culturally the distorted scientist Ideal, which wants to control, dominate and conceptually manipulate, and which is inherent to global capitalist ideology, has long been the dominant influence, shaping our institutions right into the present. The Freedom Ideal has always occupied more of a minority position. (Just as in psychotherapy Cognitive-Behavioural therapy has been and is more dominant than the Humanistic therapies). It is laughable, therefore, if not astounding, to hear educated, rational people moaning and groaning and crusading against progressive education that is taking over and destroying our schools and our nation. What is one to think of such lack of understanding? Today we can see a continuum from Back-to-Basics schooling to Traditional Education to solid renewal programs to some examples of schools with an integrated curriculum. I am not sure if there are any "Freedom" schools left. During the '70's there was a SEED alternative high-school and Magoo Elementary School. One has been transformed and the other is gone.

But, again, if the debate was really about educational practice we could sit down together and figure out where the Back-to-Basics *could* fit into a more "balanced" approach. Every approach, no matter how extreme or one-sided, has a "nugget of gold" hidden within it. It appeals to some truth. Back-to-Basics mostly champions behaviouristic methods of teaching, like programmed instruction, positive reinforcement, cues and feedback, explicit teaching, incentives, rewards and competition. Here we are in the neighbourhood of Skinner and associates. However abhorrent the behaviouristic view of reality may be to us, the true state of affairs it is appealing to is the concrete phenomenon of *habit forming* and "conditioning." In a calm debate we could probably come to a joint conclusion about when "habit forming", "conditioning", practice and mastery are appropriate and necessary within a meaningful context. Right now, given the polarized positions, this is nearly impossible.

Traditional education has been and is often the dominant influence. It is what we know from our own childhood; it is familiar and comfortable. Anything that deviates from this can make us nervous and insecure. But traditional education is in an uncomfortable position because it can end up doing neither the basics very well nor promote a meaningful context. It is certainly not the best schooling that could be. Over the decades in Ontario there has been a slow movement towards effective education. That movement needs a lot of support by the community, parents, grandparents and a lot of encouragement and training for teachers. The goal of this quiet development is to engage students in more active, genuine, lasting and meaningful learning. Change does not happen by drastic reforms without planning. Such reform is bound to fail and the signs are already there. Real change involves a process, carefully planned and supported. It is a process of continuous development and renewal. Real changes that are lasting happen step by step and require time and training of teachers to take hold and implement. The only thing that can be done quickly in education is damage.

Let me take a moment to offer an example of what often is and what could be. Let us imagine a lesson on measurement. In one class the teacher brings in some rulers, tapes and other measuring devices. She explains a little about the history of ways of measuring, the metric system and how the ruler allows measuring things in both inches and centimetres. Then after the talk, she gives the students some assignments in estimating and measuring; including some worksheets to finish at home. Time is running out and they must move on to the next lesson in a language arts workbook on word analysis, which will also have to be finished at home. She is covering the concepts and skills that are mandatory for this grade. The worksheets allow her to mark the students' achievement. Father notices that his son has a Level Two on the attached evaluation sheet. When he asks why, his son tells him he didn't get the estimating. And indeed when he looks at it the answers are wild guesses. They spend the evening estimating, walking around in dad's old shoes because they are about one foot in length. At that point the father has become the teacher's aid. It is called downloading. The curriculum guide basically holds the students and parents responsible for any failures.

Now imagine another class that is based on understanding and skill. A first grade teacher shoves the desks aside on Monday morning. With masking tape she makes an outline of a large boat on the floor. "It's the Mayflower," she says, the ship that they have been learning about.

"She hands a piece of paper to a student named Zeb and says that it is a message from the King. Zeb reads aloud that the ship can't sail until we tell the king how big it is. "What should we do?" the teacher asks. "Who has an idea?" After some false starts and some painful silences, a boy named Tom volunteers that it can't be three feet because he knows (having just been measured by the nurse) that he is four feet and the boat looks bigger than he is. Other children now join in, one suggesting that they find out how many times Tom can fit in the boat. It turns out the boat is four Toms long. Problem solved! But wait a minute, says the teacher. How will the king know what that means? After all, he's never met Tom. She waits for someone to remember that Tom is four feet tall. No one does. Instead, Mark suggests that the boat can be measured with hands. He does this several times (rather sloppily) and gets a different answer each time. After more discussion, the class realizes that you have to start right at the end of the boat and then make sure there's no space between your hands when you put them down. Finally Mark concludes to everyone's satisfaction that the boat is thirty-six hands long. Done! Well, just to be sure, says the teacher, let's have sue (the smallest child in the class) measure it again. Oh, no! Now the boat is forty-four hands long! Confusion and animated discussion follow. The children realize that all hands on deck are not of equal length. By the time someone proposes using people's feet instead, time has run out. But the teacher has them return to the problem the following day. One child now remembers that the king knows Zeb and argues that the boat can therefore be measured in multiples of Zeb's foot. The class is so excited by this that they decide to use Zeb to measure everything in the room, and the teacher lets them. It isn't until the next day, returning to the topic yet again, that she begins to make the lesson explicit to them. She invites the children to think about the importance of a standard form of measurement. And only after that does she finally introduce them to the use of rulers."[2]

---

[2] Alfie Kohn, *Schools our Children Deserve*, p.134)

She doesn't correct their mistakes. She doesn't single out certain ideas for praise. She listens and watches. She puts a further question. She stimulates learning by making problems more complex. She challenges the children to think harder and better. The lesson is hands on. The children are grappling with the *idea* of a ruler. What's more: they're *inventing* the idea of a ruler and standard measurement.

Again one may still wonder. What about the facts? Isn't it more effective to give them the facts and test them on it? An understandable response. But think again. It all depends on what kind of knowledge you would like your children to acquire: information (that may not penetrate very deeply) or personal integrated knowledge they carry with them through life?

Meanwhile I can understand how one might be uneasy with all the negative talk about public education. Why is the government and the corporate world so interest in this "Reform" that is being pushed and enforced from the outside and throwing its weight behind the first approach?

Table 7

Opposite and Conflicting Ideals for Education
(Historical, Cultural Perspective)

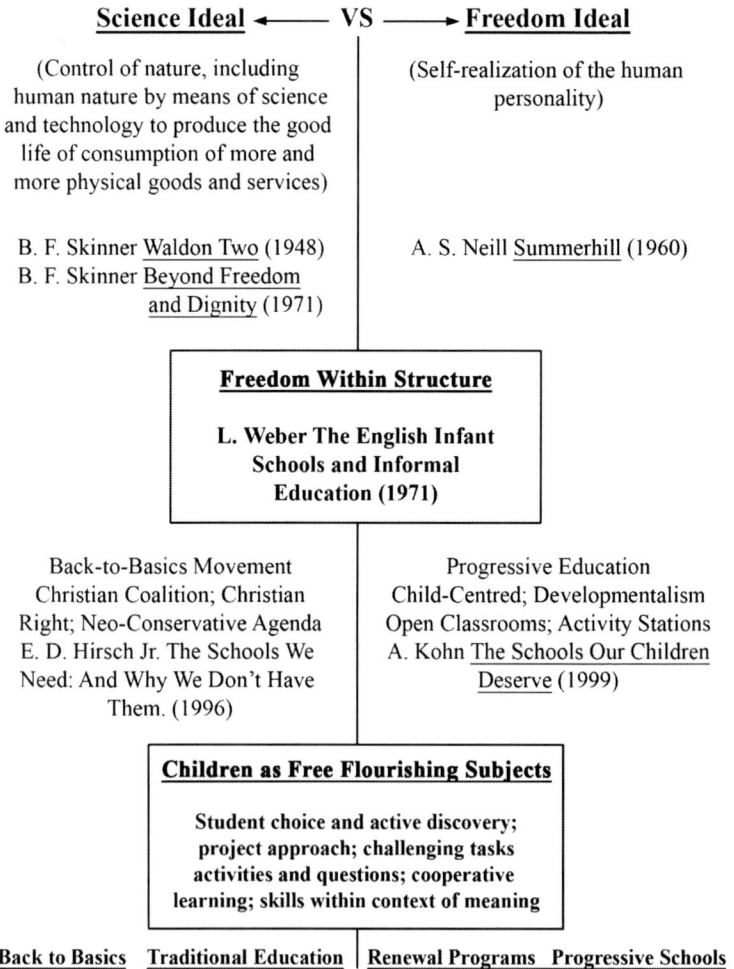

Science Ideal ◄——— VS ———► Freedom Ideal

(Control of nature, including human nature by means of science and technology to produce the good life of consumption of more and more physical goods and services)	(Self-realization of the human personality)
B. F. Skinner Waldon Two (1948) B. F. Skinner Beyond Freedom and Dignity (1971)	A. S. Neill Summerhill (1960)

Freedom Within Structure

L. Weber The English Infant Schools and Informal Education (1971)

Back-to-Basics Movement Christian Coalition; Christian Right; Neo-Conservative Agenda E. D. Hirsch Jr. The Schools We Need: And Why We Don't Have Them. (1996)	Progressive Education Child-Centred; Developmentalism Open Classrooms; Activity Stations A. Kohn The Schools Our Children Deserve (1999)

Children as Free Flourishing Subjects

Student choice and active discovery; project approach; challenging tasks activities and questions; cooperative learning; skills within context of meaning

Back to Basics   Traditional Education | Renewal Programs   Progressive Schools

5

The Changes Introduced by the Government

To get a sense of the enormity and massiveness of the educational "reform" implemented by the government we need to look at what it has done until now with such fury. The government have enacted four major changes. In sum, they have:

1) Centralized nearly all power in the Ministry of Education
2) Introduced a new funding formula
3) Introduced a new curriculum, report cards and tests
4) And to find acceptance for these changes, they have created a crisis, spread myths about the condition of our educational system and in doing so they have exploited the insecurities of the public and our fears about the future.

1) Firstly, the provincial government has centralized virtually all power in the ministry and decentralized its responsibility. A very neat trick. To accomplish this they have amalgamated the school boards and cut the number of trustees. The government capped their salaries at five-thousand dollars a year (strangling those with a lower income so that only the well-off need to run). Since all funding and curriculum decisions are now made by the ministry, boards have little actual power. The government has created large bureaucracies, quite removed from the local schools and concerns. There is evidence that smaller boards cost less and are more effective. And in downloading responsibility, the government has left school boards with the onerous task of cutting services and resources with mountains of paperwork and a maze of funding regulations. Centralized power or monopoly is in and democracy is out. All the while we're made to think that the educational reform was about greater accountability, higher standards, more involvement of parents, and so on. The opposite is true.

Meanwhile the newly created, unelected Educational Improvement Commission (1995) has been given unlimited power. On the local level the mandatory School Councils made up of parents and community members have yet to be presented with a clear mandate and, in turn, have no real power. They are left to busy themselves with fundraising and inconsequential issues. In some other provinces, however, the School Councils have already been charged with hiring and firing principals, choosing textbooks and determining teaching methods. These volunteer parent councils, no matter how dedicated, are not elected by the public and cannot be held accountable to the public. In this way, the ownership of the schools is slowly moved from general public to a private group of parents and citizens. A clever move, because it is an essential part of the privatization of public education. Once the parents are responsible and have to organize their own local "franchise", the general public is no longer involved and has no democratic representation and power. In these ways the ability to control publicly funded education in a democratic way is being reduced drastically.

2) Secondly, a new funding formula has been introduced. In total over one billion dollars has been cut. The funds allocated were supposed to be neutral in the sense that what was taken out would be put back in. This is not the case, far from it. There is some bridge funding for a year or so and there are many grants that require a lot of paperwork and have many restrictions. Since funding is now controlled by the Ministry of Education and the cabinet - instead of local boards – the government can dispense money as it sees fit. In terms of local spending on education Ontario is tenth among the provinces and territories, including the Atlantic Provinces. As one of the more corporatized of the provinces, it is a race to the bottom. The education system in Ontario is being starved of funds. You could call it: death by hunger. Usually that takes a while. Starved of funds, the deterioration of the Ontario public school system will come about slowly, dying each year a little more.

Needless to say, the consequences have already been disastrous. The Dufferin Board of Education as well as the Separate School Board, along with seventeen other boards, is in an unenviable position. Their previous spending level (in terms of cost per square foot) is quite a bit above the low average the government has set for the province. One size, one formula fits all

– and without regard for local differences (quality of buildings; heating costs; wage differences; distances for bus routes; etc.). This means that the newly amalgamated Board covering Dufferin and Wellington must cut their budget drastically. The average per square foot costs across the provinces was six dollars and forty-six cents. The new formula only allows for five dollars and twenty cents. This means that at least twenty previous boards have to scramble and cut and cut and cut and cut, which is exactly what they have been and will continue to be doing. And this is true not only for maintenance but for the other aspects of funding as well. The result is as follows:

- Neighbourhood schools will have to be closed; or twinned;
- Secretarial help is cut back; (one teacher now types her own exams or else she has to pay twenty dollars an hour for extra secretarial help);
- Teacher assistances; school psychologists; social workers; consultants; specialists; all have had to be reduced greatly;
- Library services – budgets and librarians – cut back;
- Physical education; music; art; shop teachers; all have been reduced greatly;
- Supply teachers have also been reduced or eliminated altogether (the regular teachers now have to fill in for a sick colleague and give up precious preparation time);
- Bussing services are more limited; for some children this means one-hour to one-hour and a half long bus trips;
- Special education services and teachers have been cut back and with disastrous consequences;
- School counsellors have been reduced;
- Educational programs for students at risk - cut back;
- Custodial services have been reduced;
- Adult education programs and services (a lifeline for many adults) drastically reduced;
- Textbooks and supplies have also been cut back;
- Many classes are increased to over thirty students even though the average for a board is supposed to be twenty-five; however there is no funding for more teachers;

- Despite being overworked, there has been no real increase in teachers' salaries over the last eight years
- And this is only the short of it; please see People for Education for more information.

After a few more years the educational system will start to show signs of deterioration. How could it not? It will become far less than what our children deserve – a second-rate system. Then the government has achieved its goal. In 1999 there were twenty-seven hundred classroom teachers less in Ontario than the previous year. At the same time there was a fifteen percent increase in families sending their children to private schools. The government policy is working.

6

The Consequences for Teachers

Besides the changes in funding and control with all of its consequences for the operation of the schools, the government has hastily introduced a new curriculum, new report cards and testing in grades three, six and ten. And for high school many of these changes are still being introduced. Textbooks were not available until two days before school started; this year in grade nine Science, for example, there were no Teacher Guide Books, no student workbooks, and no report cards to know what kind of evaluation was expected. Even now it is not clear what kind of foundation grade nine and ten need to lay for grades eleven and twelve. We have already looked at the elementary school curriculum: the empty curriculum; the many fragmented, distorted and developmentally inappropriate expectations with veneer of abstract scientism thrown in. But here, too, for many of the expectations there are no textbooks, units, lessons, activity books or materials to go with it. So every month there are all kinds of workshops to help teachers to work with the new curriculum. But as one teacher said: "it makes me even more discouraged, because I can't do it all. There is no time. So, I don't even look at the materials when I come home."

Then there are the new report cards. They take many teachers three weeks to write up. During that time there is very little time for any other preparation. Every report card means three weeks wasted classroom time, and all for a report that many parents don't appreciate. That is nine weeks out of the school year. For the rest of the school year many teachers put in long hours every morning and weekend, scrambling to assemble new lessons to fit the new curriculum. No wonder many teachers are stressed beyond their limits. Imagine if you have a split grade and have double sets of lessons to prepare, which is becoming increasingly common.

Many principals do not fare any better. They are snowed under by administrative work. Master teachers or principal teachers have become managers and administrators. They are now part of management and it is their job to implement the decisions of the board, deal with the cutbacks and try to maintain some semblance of morale among the teachers. No wonder many quit or are retiring early – a tremendous loss of many experienced educators to the system. As we heard on the CBC radio in an interview with principals across Canada a few months ago, many are leaving education altogether and boards are having a hard time recruiting new ones. After a while, however, that will be the local school council's job: to find their own manager principal.

And the teachers are in the same kind of bind. Let me read you a letter from one of them:

"I used to enjoy teaching. I had a meaningful program, the kids were involved, and we had help for the children who had problems. Now I just shut my door. I go through the motions. We hurry through the day. Meanwhile I am trying to figure out if I can last another ten years to early retirement. I don't think I can last that long. One of my colleagues had a breakdown. She took it all too personal. She is too dedicated, too responsible. I guess it is good for counsellors and doctors. I know of several colleagues who are on medication now. But like I said, I just shut my door. I don't know who I can talk to anymore. My principal is on the other side, now. He is part of management. We all shut our doors because I think we are all afraid and ashamed to have others see how we are trying to survive and cope. I certainly am not proud of it. It goes against my deepest grain of what I know it is to be a good teacher. I see some of the younger teachers that don't have a lot of experience. One of them always leaves at four. She never does any work at home in the evening and only does some preparing on the weekend for the coming week. She has lots of worksheets and workbooks. I can't do it that way. It is time I quit, I guess. Maybe I'll go work at Wal-Mart and worry about my pension later."

There are many teachers who feel likewise.

Regardless of whether or not you agree with the government's Reform, the way it has gone about implementing the changes is indefensible and irresponsible. The authors of *Crisis in the Classroom* describe a similar situation in the sixties and seventies and attribute the kind of irresponsibility that we are presently witnessing to mindlessness and utter stupidity.

We know of course that there is much more to it than incompetent bungling. There is another agenda that does not care about incompetence. Nevertheless, it takes a lot of gall to introduce massive changes all at once, from the top down without regard for the consequences. This is tantamount to introducing an outdated, lock-step program from grade one to eight without the upper grades having had the previous steps. When confronted by this difficulty, the education ministry has responded by saying: "well, maybe they have to take summer school." If any CEO would set about re-structuring and downsizing his corporation in this manner he would be fired within a month. For the implementation of the changes the government gets a Level Two grade, which means in terms of judging our children that they are "at risk of failure." The primary reason schools are functioning as well as they are is because of the sane, responsible, common sense principals and teachers who know how to take all of this absurdity with a grain of salt. Stressed to the limits they manage regardless of the ministry's bungling and cutting of essential and supportive services. It also says something about the strength of the educational system. It cannot be undone in a few years.

7

The Consequences for Students

This reform if enforced will automatically lead to a return to the worst aspects of traditional education. That is why I titled this presentation "Backwards into the Future." It is back-to-basics: direct teaching of facts and skills; lots of worksheets and workbooks; an emphasis on grades and testing; competition and drills; an emphasis on "right" answers; memorization; passive students; lots of homework – more of the same-tracking; retention; and so on. To make things worse this curriculum is more class-biased (economically) and culturally-biased than ever before in Ontario. No wonder things like cheating have become a more widespread problem from grade school to university. Since it sounds familiar to us it is not hard to marshal public support for it.

It is a funnel view of learning; the teacher pours in the facts while the students are told to take it in and regurgitate the contents at appropriate times. The new curriculum with its countless little low-level expectations and skills encourages and fits right in with the worst of the traditional approach. The kind of evaluations that are given, often on a daily basis (Level one, two, three, and four), and the kinds of testing encourage this approach. These kinds of tests have strong negative effects on learning. As a lot of evidence shows, it creates a preoccupation with the right answers, with how well they are doing. The impact is deep, direct and personal and it is our children this is happening to. And the more they are hurried through the day from one content to another with lots of worksheets, the more external the evaluation, the less they learn and the more external to their lives it becomes. As one second grade student said about missing a morning at school: "No, I don't mind. My teacher keeps making us work so hard and we have to hurry, and get ready for next year." When asked what they had to get ready for, he said: "I don't know." Then when asked: "Well, is someone important coming, like the Queen?" He replied, "Yes, with tests!" Refusing to let your children participate in this kind of evaluation and testing is one way to oppose this whole approach. It strikes at the core of the new curriculum. And the best research of many decades is on your side. I have carefully looked at the counter arguments and found them unsubstantiated and superficial and sometimes even downright sloganeering without any evidence. Standardized tests do not give us an accurate picture of what students really know.

A special education teacher with a lot of experience, who supervised the grade six testing last year, sent me a copy of the tests. He wrote a careful critique of the tests for his colleagues and principal. Some of his conclusions were as follows: that the validity and reliability of the tests is suspect; many of the test items were unclear or inconsistent; the scores show an abnormal distribution, which strongly suggests a defective instrument; the vocabulary was unclear, obtuse, vague or outside the students' experience at times. There are many printing defects and errors, which reflects poor planning. Many of the exercises were ill-conceived and were not adequately field tested.

His conclusions are in keeping with that of many others. Moreover, as he summarized, it encourages a very superficial treatment of the curriculum. A couple of weeks ago he noticed that teachers are already suspending their normal program and are beginning to "teach to the test" for the testing period this spring. It is clear that the Education Quality and Accountability Office have bought into a very narrow view of testing. It focuses on only one approach to problem solving, while in fact there are several other ways (cf. H. Gardener, *Multiple Intelligences*, 1994). As a result it does not measure achievement adequately. It measures only a very small segment of the students' knowledge. Instead it resembles a sort of poorly designed intelligence test (and even then it only focuses on one kind of intelligence) rather than achievement. All of this from an agency that has a budget of fifteen-million a year. Each round of testing costs about one-million to administer. A very profitable venture, indeed. It seems the EQAO knows that the testing is not going very well, that parents are beginning to object and that there are many flaws in the tests. To counter these reactions they are organizing parent workshops titled: "How to prepare your child for the test." The grade three teachers have received a "Sample Assignment Unit" so that they can teach their students how to take tests! Even some pro-reform organizations realize that the tests are inadequate. They suggest the government use some established standardized tests. But developing a good standardized test – even given its limitations – is very difficult.

We have every reason as parents to send the results right back to the ministry with the message: "No, thank you. Perhaps when you do your homework and develop a meaningful achievement test that reflects a well-rounded view of knowledge, we will reconsider letting our children participate again."

Publishing the scores of the tests in the newspapers makes things even worse and tends to lead to "unethical" practices, such as: exempting certain students that other schools may include; or by prompting and explaining questions to students. For no matter how valid the reasons, who wants to have a low score and have that published? (Lower scores consistently correlate with poverty and other non-school factors and not with the nature or quality of teaching).

In sum, we could say that standardized tests measure the wrong skills; distort classroom instruction; falsely reassure parents; and discriminate against minority and special needs students. It kills motivation and interest in learning. Tests always imply a particular kind of knowledge.

The same is true for "more of the same" kind of homework. There is no evidence of any kind that it makes any difference in students' performance on tests. Homework usually means more mindless busy work. As one famous researcher put it: "there are many ways to measure a successful school – the creativity of the students, their happiness, their hunger to learn new things, their love of reading. But at this point in our history, the most important measure is performance on standardized tests. As long as that is true, those backpacks are likely to be full each night starting in grade one and maybe earlier." So if your children don't have homework of the usual kind that may just be a cause for celebration and for engaging your kids in some meaningful learning of things that interest them at home. If your school scores low on the standardized test there is reason to look at all the non-school factors like poverty that may be influencing the results and to see if anything can be done in the community. As it stands now, schools with a low score will be "punished" and will get a year or so to pull up their average. So they will need to learn to be inventive or subversive.

We have a thirty year more or less progressive stream of education here in Ontario that many international visiting educators have envied. Starting with the Hall-Dennis report in 1968, the reports in 1975 and 1984, slowly on in this development some of the pitfalls of child-centered learning, like open classrooms, inadequate assessment and teacher training have balanced out. It is only in 1995 when the NDP government introduced an outcomes-based program called *The Common Curriculum* (grades one to nine) that the Trojan horse entered the schools even though it was still partly couched in progressive educational language. All the conservative government had to do was complete the job while maintaining some of the progressive language. Had it been the liberal government the same would have probably happened. The statements in the Red Book and that of different liberal cabinet ministers; their endorsement of "partnerships" between industry and education; their view of the alignment of the goals of education with those of the global market economy; their view of the knowledge industry as an export commodity; their repetitions of the myths about education – all of that makes it quite plain and clear where the liberals stand. I am not, however, clear where the NDP stand at this point. Regardless, what is clear is that real development and progress in education as well as in society on a whole will be up to us.

8

The Government and Corporate Agenda

Why would the government along with big business want to do this? What is at stake for them? Why would they put a public school system at risk?

There seem to be *two* reasons that motivate the government. The first is to take money from health care, social services and education in order to finance their promised tax cuts. In other words, more than a century old public school system is put at risk for short-term political gain. Secondly, there is a strong push to privatize education and to open it up to the "free market". As one analyst of the First Canadian Education Industry Summit said in 1997: "Canadian schools are ripe for the picking." They are worth billions of dollars in business. It assumes a market model of education: compete in the open market; introduce "choice", preferably character schools and a voucher system; let schools compete for customers; consumer power will ensure that everyone gets what he or she is willing or able to pay. The consequences of this ideology are a two level or two-tier educational system, like in New Zealand, Australia, England and some places in the United States and Alberta. On the one hand, there will be the private schools and the well-off public schools that can offer better services, and then there will be the second-rate schools in poorer areas – or what are termed the "sink" schools in England – on the other. If you want to see the results of privatization then look at these examples, or, here in Ontario, at in what direction and how fast the *Ontario Coalition for Educational Reform* want the government to move. Schools are under attack not because they are failing, but because they are public. In our increasingly multicultural society the public school system is more important than ever and worth defending. It is one important place where children from different backgrounds can learn to understand and respect each other. This struggle is not only about our public schools but about all public institutions that are under democratic control and that function to meet peoples' needs and not those of corporations and shareholders.

In order to sell this ideological agenda to the public, as I have already alluded, the government had to create a crisis and repeat a number of myths about our educational system. It required a lot of propaganda, wheelbarrows full, costing millions of tax dollars. As one full page advertisement stated: "Our education system isn't working! Our children are falling behind." Dozens of these kinds of statements have been reported and repeated over and over in the press. The general theme is usually the following:

Our students' knowledge needs to be upgraded if we are going to be able to compete in the global market. Otherwise we are at risk of falling behind. We need to improve our student's literacy, numeracy and critical thinking ability. This concern echoes a widespread conviction in the business world and in the public in general that graduates are not measuring up; we are falling behind; we won't have the skilled workforce we need to be able to keep up in the technology-driven global economy. In this climate a number of myths about education and our schools have been invented, passed on and repeated over and over again even though they have no basis in fact. These are some of the myths:

(1) Our schools have failed us and our children.

- It is propagated that at least twenty-five percent of Canadians are illiterate, when the actual figure is around three percent of Canadian born youth between sixteen and twenty-four. In fact, illiteracy relates to disability, illness, poverty, unemployment, family chaos, etc. and not first of all to our schools. In turn, against the governments' propaganda, library use has nearly doubled in Canada and tripled in Quebec.

- It is claimed that our drop-out rate is at least thirty percent. On the contrary, the drop-out rate is around eighteen percent and slowly decreasing as attested by the fact that in 1971 it was forty-eight percent and in 1956 the drop-out rate was seventy percent. Again, it should also be pointed out that drop-out rates relate to social factors, first.

- The government claims that we spend more on education than any other country in the world, and we have less to show for it. It also claims that we waste money on huge bureaucracies and overpaid teachers. But in truth, Canada is actually forth lowest out of twenty countries when it comes to how much is spent on elementary and secondary education; and in terms of proportion spent on teachers' salaries, Canada ranks seventh out of twelve. As I have state previously, teachers haven't had a real pay raise for the last eight years.

- It is claimed that students in all countries with which Canada competes work harder and longer. In Japan and Germany kids go to school two-hundred and forty-three and two-hundred and forty days as opposed to children in Canada who go to school roughly one-hundred and eighty-five days a year. The truth however is that the aforementioned figure with regards to Japanese students also includes festive, sport and cultural days, while the school day itself is much shorter. Canadian students actually are exposed to more hours of instruction – nine-hundred and fifty-two hours compared to nine-hundred and thirty-three for Japanese students.

- It is also said that our students' performance in international competitions falls below almost all other countries, while in reality our students perform as well on average as those of most other countries. It should also be noted that more often than not international competitions and tests compare very different student populations and programs of study; interpreting results from international competitions has become a science in itself.

(2) Our graduates don't have the skills required to compete in a global economy.

- With regards to this point it is said that there is a labour force shortage. The reality is that there tends to be an oversupply of scientists and engineers; and that Canada ranks among the top five of industrial countries when measuring workers' skills and first among G7 countries in annual per capita science and engineering degrees.

- The government also claims that when statistics are quoted about skilled labour shortages we better inquire about the source of those figures, when Canada does not even have a way of accurately measuring trends and expectations in jobs such as exists in the United States. Information has to be culled together from many different sources.

(3) The government is fond of the claim that big business is creating highly skilled jobs, especially in the knowledge intensive industries.

- On the contrary, the fact is that a permanent restructuring and distribution of jobs has taken place, which has resulted in a new structural unemployment and underemployment.
- There are actually very few signs of major developments in the knowledge intensive industries.
- Likewise, instead of redesigning production processes requiring higher skills, capitalist industry has taken recourse to restructuring, downsizing, rolling back wages; out-sourcing; and moving production to countries with low-skilled labour force, lower taxes, low labour conditions and protection and low environmental standards.
- The result of this is that the bulk of new jobs are low-skilled and that eighty percent of all jobs require no more than a grade eight education. Generally speaking, most workers are overqualified and underutilized. Five of the most highly skilled occupations only make up six percent of all jobs.

As if coming to terms with all the government deceit was not enough, all of this means that millions of young people in Canada are being trained for jobs that don't exist or won't exist where they live. The myths hold up the big carrot and the big stick. If you study hard there will be a bright future for you, if not, you only have yourself to blame. What a hoax being played on our children and young people.

Corporate leaders everywhere are perpetuating these myths and scapegoating the public school system. When confronted by the facts, a representative of the Conference Board of Canada, for example, which is made up of the one-hundred largest corporations doing business in Canada, said that the

Conference Board would stand by its charges not because they were factual but because it was what their members believed. What do you do with such disinformation, misrepresentation, distortions, or outright deception? Apparently both big business, through its many organizations and think tanks as well as many individual leaders and the government, whether conservative or liberal, feel free to bash schools and teachers. They in fact have become more and more brazen, shameless, obscene and dishonest in their statements. What are we to think of a corporate representative warning the participants of an Educational Industry Summit in 1997 with Sergio Marchi, the then trade minister, present: that even though running chains of for-profit schools may seem easy, beware. It's a real snake pit of local politics out there. "Local schools are fiercely defended by hysterical middle-aged women. I call them the bitch-ilanties." What are we to think of such shamelessness and brazenness? I am a senior, quiet, introverted male. What would this person label me? If middle-aged women are called bitches because they object to the commercialization of education, I guess they might call me a "senile, old son of a bitch."

The constant repetition of these myths by corporate and government leaders and corporate controlled mainstream media creates a deep anxiety and makes many parents nervous about their children's education and future. They prey on this anxiety, an anxiety that is really caused by economic uncertainty, restructuring and downsizing. Education is an easy target. It makes parents doubt and say: well, if that is the problem, let's go back to the basics and raise the standards.

9

The Corporate Vision of Life

Why is education suddenly of such concern to business and capitalist industry, especially the corporate leaders and their organizations? When corporations plan a take-over their target is rarely a company without worth but one that is valuable and vulnerable. They have a lot at stake. The best I have been able to gather from many different sources is that the corporate world has its own vision of life. It is the dominant vision of life in the Western world and on our continent. In as much as we all participate in this vision and way of life, it also means that we are all part of the problem, whether we are Christians, Roman Catholic or Protestant; Jewish; Muslim; Hindu; Buddhist; Humanist; Post Modernist; Native People or whatever else our convictions may be. We all live more or less split lives in our culture. This means we cannot just denounce corporations, although that may be tempting at times. For when we are critical of the corporate vision of life, we are by implication critical of ourselves, for we all participate in that vision and way of life. The trans-national corporations do embody this vision of life most clearly; but so do we in our addiction to consumerism. Christmas is not far behind us.

What is this vision and way of life? In its extreme, as an ideology, a belief system, it has to do with reducing life to becoming producers and consumers. Whatever can be made must be made regardless of the consequences for the environment, labour conditions, our general health, the meaningfulness of work, and so on. Happiness is the consumption of more and more and always new physical goods and services. It is a one-dimensional view of life and of this world of our experience. Life as with experience is reduced to its economic dimension, to an endless mode of exploitation and consumption of goods. It involves the commercialization of all of life – nothing can be excluded. The free market must reign supreme.

It gives rise to intense competition; ruthless takeovers; a totally free, deregulated market and the elimination of all barriers to the free flow of capital. This requires a remodelling of society by means of privatizing and restructuring. Public democratic institutions and agencies stand in the way of the "free market". Public assets must be sold off. You could call it a new form of Social Darwinism – survival of the fittest; as well as an extreme individualism. As Margaret Thatcher once said: "there is no such thing as society, just individuals and families." That is to say that we are all just "utility maximizers". We have no altruistic or community motives, only selfish ones. So people must slowly be weaned away from their commitment to community, cooperation and care. It makes for a harsher people and society, one that is less compassionate and less responsible for each other. You could call this view a rationalization of one tendency in human nature – greed and selfishness – and ignoring the other tendencies toward altruism and empathy, toward care and a sense of responsibility for each other – of community. It is the opposite of a multidimensional view of life and many-sided values.

Table 8

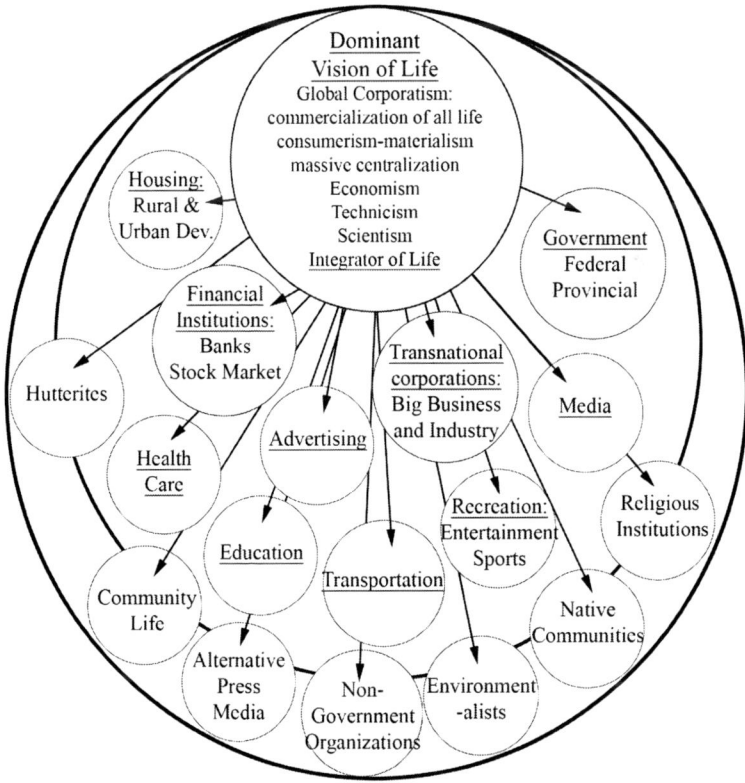

Dominant
Vision of Life
Global Corporatism:
commercialization of all life
consumerism-materialism
massive centralization
Economism
Technicism
Scientism
Integrator of Life

Housing:
Rural &
Urban Dev.

Government
Federal
Provincial

Financial
Institutions:
Banks
Stock Market

Transnational
corporations:
Big Business
and Industry

Hutterites

Media

Health
Care

Advertising

Recreation:
Entertainment
Sports

Religious
Institutions

Community
Life

Education

Transportation

Native
Communities

Alternative
Press
Media

Non-
Government
Organizations

Environment
-alists

10

The Corporate Agenda and Education

To keep selling this vision of life, corporations must have the *allegiance of the people* and particularly the young. And schools are the ideal place to indoctrinate students, to distort their worldview, and have them buy into a "free" market vision of life. Fostering the culture of competiveness in the schools undermines values of cooperation and community, of equality and democratic rights. It encourages students to accept the dog-eat-dog environment of the global economy, of competition against each other for scarce jobs; of the values of individual free enterprise and corporate loyalty. It encourages external motivation by competition and testing. Students learn to accept jumping through the hoops enticed by the carrot of high-skilled and high paying jobs (that don't exist for the majority).

Secondly, not only must schools be used to foster allegiance to corporate values, but the schools themselves must be privatized and commercialized. School children are the largest untapped consumer market in our society. Many concerned people are tracing this corporate intrusion into the educational system, particularly by means of advertising, offering so-called partnerships, and of providing curriculum materials.

On the wall here is a list of corporations providing curriculum materials for us in the schools. Imagine Mobil, Exxon, Shell, etc. providing fair and in-depth materials on the environment, pollution and sustainable development. Meanwhile, the environment content of the new scientisitic curriculum (fifty-two out of eight-hundred and sixty-five expectations) has been reduced to six percent. As one teacher has said, "the study of the societal implications of any topic has been relegated to a special term project because of lack of time." So much for lip service to sustainable development, environmental protection and conservation in the curriculum.

Thirdly, perpetuating the myths about education and pressuring for the reform of the school system also provides business and industry with a docile, cooperative future workforce, willing to jump through the hoops. Overproduction of qualified young people gives great advantage to employers. As long as education is presented as giving an edge in the job market, students will compete for high-skilled jobs. And as long as some are perceived to attain this goal and the others are willing to strive for the top, all is well. If everyone had a PhD however, there would still be over one-half of a million people unemployed or more and at least one million under-employed persons as well as many millions in boring, mindless poorly paid jobs. Such is the hoax. But it does provide the business world with a reliable supply of adaptable, flexible, loyal, mindful, expendable and "trainable" workers.

The subtle and not so subtle training in the corporate culture is the *real center of the empty curriculum*. As a result we have a generation of children "growing up corporate" – as consumers in training. This indoctrination of the dominant corporate vision of life happens partly through the content of the curriculum and the parts that are missing – the questions that are not asked – and partly through the way the school and learning are structured – testing and competition as well as the promotion of a highly distorted way of being – the medium is the message. No doubt many schools and many teachers still find their way around this indoctrination to soften its impact. However, there are many examples in the U.S. where this kind of schooling is enforced – where teaching methods, facts and skills, drills and tests are prescribed by legislation and where teachers have to sign that they will teach in the prescribed manner.

Much more could be said about this trend. But many others have written about it and we have detoured enough to get back to the curriculum, children's learning and their testing. The real debate is not about testing, homework, a return to the three R's, higher standards, traditional vs. Progressive teaching and learning – nor is it about a phonetic approach to reading or whole language. It is a debate about two sets of values, two visions of life. It is a split that we may also recognize in ourselves. A battle between a life-enhancing view of the world and a life-distorting vision. Moreover, it is a battle between a reductionistic, overly conceptualized and abstract one-dimensional view of life and a multidimensional view in which all aspects of life have their rightful place. It is therefore a difference between seeing ourselves primarily as a consumer or as an autonomous, free flourishing subject, partner, neighbour, parent, citizen, homemaker, environmental-caretaker, promoter of emotional and physical well-being, music lover, artist, decorator, sports person, and so on. The Hebrew Scriptures call it *Shalom*: everything having its rightful place under the sun providing for what it is called to do, which creates harmony and peace. Perhaps this is what makes these debates about educational issues so vehement and fierce. It also makes it hard to discuss these issues in a calm and reasonable way, carefully weighing the evidence.

11

The Consequences for the High-School Curriculum

Presently, the high-school curriculum is also being brought in line with the corporate and government agenda. Most of the big trade organizations like MAI, NAFTA, APEC, WTO, OECD, through their think tanks, working groups and conferences have issued major reports on education. The stakes are high. One such paper, an APEC position paper, makes it very clear that:

- Schools are the global engines of human resource development;
- Education for itself or for good citizens is no longer appropriate;
- Learning for the sake of learning is wasteful;
- Non-productive education must be eliminated;
- Work as just an instrumental part of life reflects an unacceptable dichotomy;
- The goals of education must be subjected to global market forces;
- Decisions must be made for good business reasons with maximum business intervention

Many trans-national corporations also have their own mission statements about education and have committed millions of dollars for the development of curriculum materials, teacher training, scholarships, awards, and programs for parents, etc. As the Dow Chemical literature puts it so succinctly: "Only a fraction of the students will become scientists and engineers, but all students – and society – benefit from a thorough technical education. These students become the voters and consumers who will buy our products and who will go to the polling booth and vote on issues that affect the success of our industry." For that reason Parental Involvement is one of the three areas eligible for funding. However, most importantly, specific reforms must address the structure and curriculum of the schools', the quality and certification of instructors, and standard requirements. It is about "rethinking and redesigning education and whole-school change," as the Panasonic Foundation puts it. In keeping with this view, corporations provide "balanced perspectives on environmental issues ...without finger-pointing or blame placing," as well as on many other issues.

The skills and attitudes that corporations expect is even more directly and specifically formulated by the J. C. Penny Corporation, ninety-two expectations to be exact. The Conference Board of Canada in their Employability Skills Profile list twenty-six expectations. The new Ontario high-school curriculum is being brought in line with the corporate demands and expectations.

As a result of such views and demands education is increasingly geared to the global economy. The role of student and citizen is increasingly becoming synonymous with producer (in-training) and consumer (in-training). Thus the curriculum needs to be re-tooled to better sort and train students and prepare them for their role in the global market. If you look at the new high-school curriculum from this perspective, the changes all make sense. Sorting and streaming from grade eight and on. Students have to choose right away in grade nine whether to take academic or applied courses. Only twenty to twenty-five percent is expected to go on to university. The rest of the students will be "prepared" for the workplace through cooperative education, apprenticeship programs, courses in learning strategies and career studies. They will be followed closely and made to jump through the hoops. School must prepare for the workplace and as Dow Chemical puts it: to become an informed and loyal customer. A middle group can take college preparation courses for more intermediate, lower-level technical and skill programs.

In this light let us look at the Technological Education courses. The old Media "literacy" and "awareness" course has been changed. It served as a little bit of protection against the approximate four-thousand commercial messages a day and made students more aware of the nature of advertising. One part of "media literacy" has been incorporated in the English programs. The emphasis, however, is on the technical aspect of media presentations. There is no expectation of dealing with the critical evaluation of the role of the media and advertising in our society. The other part of media studies is incorporated in the new Technological Education courses. Here too there is nothing about the role of the media and advertising in general in our society and the corporate control of the media. Nor is there any mention of the necessity for an alternative press and media to give some kind of coherent picture of what is happening. There is, indeed, very little concern for the context. There is only technological skill information with a small gesture to the ethics of how you use "communication technology." The same things can be said about Construction Technology, Health Technology and Personal Services Technology, Hospitality and Tourism Technology, Manufacturing Technology, and Transportation Technology. Under Health Technology one of the expectations is that students "describe the role of the health care industry locally, provincially and nationally." No mention of the life and death struggle of the health care system, the role of the drug companies, the impact of an older aging population, the impact of poverty on health; AIDS prevention; research and medications; the unhealthy diets and lifestyles of many North Americans; preventative and alternative medicine; etc. A wealth of real life issues to engage students for a whole year. It would provide a context for deciding whether or not one wants to pursue a technological career in this area. The technical training itself doesn't really take all that much. But industry only wants compliant technicians, not informed responsible citizens that have a mind of their own.

The same things can be said about the academic courses. The academic disciplines are separated from each other without overarching connections or context. Of course there is nothing wrong with pursuing an in-depth study of an academic field that does justice to the integrity of the field, whether it be mathematics or physics or philosophy or any other discipline. That can be exciting and worthwhile, as long as there is some overarching, interdisciplinary course to provide perspective. As one OISE professor put it some time ago: "By virtue of what "science" has become in the western world, the primary sciences are without self-reflection. They cannot examine themselves. Nor will they allow for the open examination of their relations to other sciences." Nor do they depend on a philosophical perspective. Or, as Postman and Weingartner state rather humorously in *Teaching as a Subversive Activity* (1969):

> "English is not History and History is not Science and Science is not Art and Art is not Music, and Art and Music are minor subjects and English, History and Science major subjects, and a subject is something you "take" and, when you have taken it you have "had" it, and if you have "had" it, you are immune and need not take it again."

As a result of dividing life according to the disciplines and having to cover all the "science" subjects, students in grade nine and ten for example have to cover units in biology, physics, chemistry, astronomy, earth sciences, ecology and technology. For both grades there is an Academic and an Applied stream. Looking at some of the textbooks and teachers' guides, I would call this a backwards approach. First the scientific concepts are explained; then students do experiments; and finally there are a number of problems and issues raised that relate to society and the environment, each of which could engage the students for a whole semester. But time is short and they must hurry to the next topic and be ready for grade twelve tests in science and mathematics and the entry requirements for university. A little term paper of no more than ten pages worth twenty percent of the final mark on biotechnology hardly makes for an integrated curriculum dealing with real-life issues.   As a part of the grade nine biology strand (Reproduction: Processes and Applications), students study Human Reproduction. There is no mention of relationships, love, respect, abuse, date-rape, sexually transmitted diseases, birth control, and so forth. There are only biological processes of fertilization. This is not exactly what preoccupies fifteen year olds if you listen to what they talk about on the phone in the evening, for hours, or the questions they ask Sue Johansan. Those topics are covered in another, unrelated course in Health and Physical Education (again as one part of four strands). The only application they are required to study is reproductive technologies, in Vitro fertilization and risk factors during pregnancy. Meanwhile, the larger context of relationships and parenting is strikingly absent.

Instead of this fragmented curriculum – a world divided according to disciplines (for the twenty-five percent that go to university) – there could be an integrated, overarching program of studies for each of the major areas of life. The resources and materials are all there as we will see in a moment.

As it stands now, the high-school curriculum has been brought in line with corporate expectations and demands of the global economy. Through the curriculum the Trojan horse has been hauled in, right into the heart of the high-school. It allows the larger corporations to scoop off the cream of the crop for the high-tech and high paying jobs and provide lower technical and skill training for the rest. For those who are unwilling or unable to compete for room at the top, they will be conditioned and pressured to accept whatever jobs are available at minimum or near minimum wage. This is the emerging class system: an upper and a lower class, and the underclass that don't count.

The students' career choices are not likely to come out of being opened up to the richness and possibilities of life and the many issues and problems that call for an insightful, enthusiastic, positive and committed young people. Career studies, business courses and technological courses hardly provide such perspectives. And what if a person's talents and interests are not primarily science, math, technology and business? Don't they count? What if their particular interests are not "profitable" in the present marketplace? Does that mean their talents are not worthwhile and are less valuable to society? The new curriculum strongly suggests that students must do everything they can to make their interest fit into a restricted marketplace and make them profitable. Artists, musicians, actors, writers, and many others in our community know all about this as they struggle to "make a living." Ironically they add more real value to our communities than yet another electronic gadget or new fast food product.

It is time that we look at some genuine alternatives and possibilities that could give our young people the kind of education they deserve. It is a choice between two visions of life; two approaches to learning. The one approach leads to understanding, to excitement, happiness, cooperation, to real ability and skill and love of learning. The other approach leads to routine, boredom, distraction, drills without any real understanding and often requires control by detentions and the threat of failure. Drugs and drinking help them survive from the hopeless and increasingly meaningless futures society offers them. After a recent shooting in Toronto, Dan Offord, director of the Canadian Centre for Studies of Children at Risk in Hamilton, Ontario said: "The problem isn't school violence. The school resides in the community. There are problems in the community. It starts small and grows. You're going to have to find ways early on, before it gathers steam and gets into the high-schools. Too many young people feel marginalized. Once you marginalize kids, you're asking for trouble. Not only are their lives miserable, they make others' lives miserable. There has to be a place for all kids."

As I asked a young graduate the other day, an average student, but a bright person: "What do you remember most about high-school? What lingers?" He replied: "not much. Very little lingers. I just went through all the motions, sort of on automatic, like I do in my job. I did the work and passed, that is all. Don't ask me what I studied because I don't remember. Now I just go to the library and pick out books that interest me. I have always done that!" How different his education could have been. What a shame and what a waste of talent, time and energy.

12

Whose Curriculum? Who Decides?

Before we look at an alternative approach, there is one more burning question. Who decides what and how our children will learn? Certainly big business and industry have no right to decide. If the corporate world showed concerted effort to develop more high-tech jobs that required a large skilled workforce and if they showed commitment to sustainable development in terms of the conservation of limited resources and environmental protection – if they showed concern for the permanent structural changes that are happening in the world of work, etc. they would have a right to have a voice in asking schools to prepare students for the kind of work they are providing, those which require more than a grade eight level of education. Right now they are mainly playing a hoax on the students and deceiving them – for their own purposes. We have little evidence of corporations wanting to monitor themselves and adhere to new labour and environmental standards and wanting to be good corporate citizens. The transnational corporations, their think-tanks, organizations and spokespersons have forfeited their right to speak, probably for decades to come.

The same is true of the government. They have a right to demand a certain level of literacy, numeracy and understanding by the time students finish high-school. An advanced democratic society requires a level of knowledge of its citizens that allow them to make intelligent decisions with regard to complex issues. Beyond that the government has no business in the classroom to dictate what will be taught and how. It can demand a certain level of knowledge, set up safety laws, and so forth; but that is all. It ought to provide the conditions so that education can be practiced freely, so that it can flourish in society. In the same way, the government have no business in our places of worship, beyond safety issues, sexual abuse, hate literature, brainwashing, mind control in certain cults, etc. It cannot dictate how you worship, when and what the content should be. Likewise, the government has no business in our bedroom. Just imagine. Most of all, the provincial and federal government have no moral authority left to speak about education or make any decisions. They have squandered that right even within their rightful domain. And whatever formal legal authority they have can easily be defeated by the counter measures of this community: citizens, parents, teachers, principals, and trustees.

So who decides on the main content of the curriculum? The answer – in my opinion – is you as parents and representatives of the community at large. That does pose a problem in a diverse and multicultural society. But it is not a problem which cannot be overcome. I dare say that if we had an all-day workshop on a Saturday, that together we could figure out what kind of knowledge and what areas of life and, in each area, what issues we would like the school to deal with. Then we can leave it to the teachers to work out what kind of units and activities they develop and to plan together and coordinate when they will deal with certain units – that is their principal expertise. This is easier than you may think. First of all there are the common areas of life.

If we brainstormed on each of these areas, I trust we would come up with a list of core values and issues that we would like the school to deal with in a fair and balanced way – that is, to look at things from all sides, consider different points of view, critically weigh the evidence – all in a spirit of care, compassion and tolerance with room for righteous indignation; and above all with a view to positive action. For we are all tempted to live split lives. The goal is to help our students develop into thoughtful, knowledgeable, caring citizens, (and not angry, powerless crusaders). Developing such a common vision for our public schools requires a lot of patience, acceptance and above all, tolerance.

For the primary grades all this is easier yet. The curriculum could just be built around the core areas of life: air, water, earth, plants, animals, family, neighbourhoods, rural and urban areas, transportation, energy and industries related to these areas of life together with some key issues and their interconnectedness in a three year cycle. I am sure there are many other ways to organize a curriculum as long as it is approached in an integrated, multidimensional, whole, real-life way. Children and youth need to be opened up to these dimensions of life that we all share. They experience birth and death; brokenness and healing; joy and sadness; they begin to discern specific instances of right and wrong; and so on. They need to be introduced to the many current issues facing them, and us, in a fair, open and responsible manner.

If it is up to us, locally, as communities, then it challenges us to gather courage and our sense of empowerment and engage in active protest, alternative action, and in "subversive" activity. As a teacher, to subvert means that you "hold down" the wrong and that you do what you consider to be good teaching and learning. It means that you engage your students in integrated, meaningful projects and that you take the time each unit requires. It means that you pay lip service to the new curriculum and to the new report cards.

It may mean that you do some isolated skill practice that won't come up right away in the unit being studied on Mondays so that you can devote the rest of the week to meaningful projects and let your students in on it to gain their cooperation. To be "subversive" in this context means that you are doing what is morally right. It means that if anyone asks you: "Are you following the new curriculum?" You look them straight in the eye and say: "Yes, of course I am." And to you that would mean: "I am doing what I think is the right thing with my students." To state the factual truth in that context would be unethical and would prevent you from doing the right thing, which so blatantly speaks in our experience with the critical realities surrounding the state of our educational system. I personally learned about this difference during the war when my father said to the soldier: "No, there are no Jews or eligible works in our house." By which he meant that there were no sub-human creatures or slave labourers hidden in our house. The man hidden between our upstairs floors was our neighbour, a fellow human. Factual truth and the real truth are not always the same.

So put the new curriculum on the shelf, pay lip service to it and most important of all, join together with other teachers and enlist parents' help. Hopefully your principal will be on your side and as a good manager will lead his or her team in a discussion of

Alfie Kohn's book, *The Schools our Children Deserve* and strategize how collectively you may bring this transformation about step by step. It would present a great opportunity to become creative and innovative together.

As a community it challenges us to support the teachers in their effort to develop a more integrated and meaningful curriculum. We can help by searching out resources and collecting or making materials. There is a lot available already. We don't have to reinvent the wheel. Parents can do something similar to the parents whose letter I read in the beginning. A copy will be available.

Board members are challenged to actively protest the decisions of the Ministry and to search out the truth about the funding formulas.

The next biggest temptation for all of us is to get co-opted and subverted into accepting the wrong and rationalizing the consequences. Unfortunately there are many examples of this as well. Money is a strong lure. As one superintendent recently stated: "it is a no-brainer. It is just such an easy way to raise a few dollars for our schools. It's the real world." He had negotiated a special deal with McDonalds so that poor kids and their families could eat there more often. Or the teacher in St. John's who reorganized her class like a corporation. The students became workers and the parents the board of governors. Then there is the Toronto School Board's Pepsi deal. Recently, Mississauga has fallen too and so many others. The corporations have made tremendous inroads already into the schools through advertising, curriculum materials, resources, teacher training, scholarships, and so on. They are like giant squids. Their tentacles reach into every aspect of the school curriculum. So when Wal-Mart offers a prize or a scholarship, beware. Or when in Simcoe County a private company called Sound Readers can use the schools to advertise their questionable, commercial reading program, it may seem innocent but that's how it happens, step by step. In a more subtle way there are the many school districts and teachers that have been enlisted to create this new Ontario curriculum. And finally as a community, who have stood by, unaware, trusting or increasingly despairing, but accepting. We are all in danger of being co-opted and subverted. It is time to stand up.

Table 6

Our Common Life-Tasks	
	-Efficacious agent
	-Partner, parent, friend
	-Citizen, worker
	-Neighbour
	-Communicator
	-Problem Solver
Our Common responsibilities or tasks:	-Maker, learner
Our roles in the different dimensions of life; the creative fulfillment of our giftedness in response to the evocativeness of life, whether life enhancing or life distorting.	-Symbolizing and being creative
	-Promoting emotional well-being
	-Promoting physical health
	-Recreation, leisure
	-Environmental care-taker
	-Managing transitions and changes
	-Promoting tolerance

13

Possibilities and Actualities

The opposite type schooling and learning can be described as progressive education, project based learning, active discovery and involvement, learner-centered, with lots of student choice and collaboration which affirms cooperative learning, different kinds of assessment and evaluation – all the things that horrify back-to-basics advocates. In such a learning environment the classroom feels like a caring community; students feel safe and valued. They trust they won't be laughed at or otherwise made to feel stupid. It creates a sense of belonging and connection and a fertile environment for learning. Year by year they are opened up to reality, to real-life situations – to the good and the bad – and are quickly nudged to embrace a life enhancing vision and way of life.

Let me give you two inspiring examples of such programs of learning. Imagine starting with a real-life, concrete phenomenon like all the rivers in this area. We live in the "Headwaters Area" – the origin of many rivers and creeks. There is the Credit River, the Grand, the Nottawasaga, the Boyne, the Pine, the Mad and the Noisy Rivers as well as Sheldon Creek with smaller tributaries. To study some of these rivers many of the topics for grade nine and ten could be included. There is actually a well-worked out, integrated series of six curriculum guides available called *Rivers* – Geography; Earth Sciences; Chemistry; Biology; Language Arts and Mathematics. They are being implemented by many schools across North America and beyond. Teacher training workshops are being offered to work with these guides and teachers and students can stay in touch via the Internet and e-mail. Imagine such an interdisciplinary, integrated study right here in Orangeville, Shelburne, Grand Valley or Alliston. In fact, it could become even more integrated over time and include issues of water tables, pollution, run-offs, preservation, water quality, weather patterns, organisms, fish, the unique geography of this area, drought, wells drying up, water scarcity, water as a commodity, art and literature, music and drama related to water and so forth. The monitoring could tie in and be passed on to the Nottawasaga Valley Conservation Authority, as well as the Credit Valley Conservation Authority, the Ministry of the Environment and the Ministry of Natural Resources, the Universities of Waterloo and Guelph, and so on. The Headwaters and the Grand River Fly Fishing Club could provide valuable information and assistance. They have many knowledgeable members. Then there is the Ontario Naturalist Society (FONS) as well as the Dufferin Forestry Association; etc. It is very near us to do. There are some excellent resources available for such a project and many people that could assist and help out.

Students can share and communicate their findings with others all over North America, and students planning to go on to university can take (an) academic course(s) as well. Technology students could connect with the Mardoo River and River Mud: Model IT multimedia programs. This integrated study would give meaning and purpose to their technological courses. For others it would open up a life-long appreciation of and awareness about our environment and the interconnectedness of everything. They would become committed to sustainable development and to the preservation of our environment for generations to come. The grade eleven and twelve students could also teach and help a grade seven and eight class, because most of the projects and testing are manageable to them. And they in turn could adopt a grade three and four class. Because there are some equally exciting programs available for that level. Just read the two accounts in the latest issue of the Green Teacher, entitled: "Ecology Project Learning" and "Streams," as well as a host of other projects; wetlands (there is an undisturbed wetland right here in Orangeville at the entrance to the town on Highway 10); Project North, The Monarch Butterfly project as well as projects on forests and everything related to forests.

There would be no need for expensive textbooks at forty dollars per title. A couple of copies would do fine as references. The thousands of dollars could be used for other resource materials.

Projects like the *River* and all others linger and last. They connect students to the Internet and to other students. In the end it prepares students for alternative jobs related to the environment and society; jobs that require more than a grade eight education. The present government can cut back on environmental and social organizations but the increasing problems won't go away and will come back with a vengeance. And that is true for most areas of our lives that have been ignored.

There are similarly exciting projects in Social Studies and History, in the Arts, in Geography, in Language Arts and Literature. We have the Dufferin County Museum with its rich resources right next door to us. When you read these examples and projects you can't help but get excited. And I have mentioned only a small part of what is available in resources. Nevertheless, it makes one want to join in and learn the things we were deprived of as children. Truth be told, it is never too late; we can all join in, in some way, in this kind of foundational and concrete learning – and for the rest of our lives.

Roy Cummings of the Boyne River Outdoor Education Centre wrote his master's thesis last year on the effects of outdoor education on students. He interviewed students from twenty years ago. He told them: "You may not remember your week at the outdoor education center, but..." And before he could finish they would interrupt him and say – "Oh, I remember exactly: on day one we did such and such, on day two..." and so on. I mentioned this to my sister-in-law Maria and she said: "I remember, I was there..." and she proceeded to tell me what they did and the lasting impression it made. If one week can have such lasting effect, imagine what a whole semester or a whole year of personal, hands-on, real-life solid work could do.

Unfortunately, since there are no funds in the education budget for outdoor centres they may all be at risk, or they may have to start fundraising like the Boyne River Ecology Centre (that is part of the Boyne River Outdoor Centre), or even start charging a fee for service, which would only create a class division.

Regardless, these Outdoor Educational Centres all around us could provide valuable information and assistance. Many of the teachers there have many years of experience at the Boyne River, the Pine River, the Mono Cliffs, the Sheldon Creek Centres and others. Then there are about forty to sixty integrated semester-long programs, which offer four credits for grades eleven and twelve students in various high-schools all over Ontario like the course in Alliston. What a wealth of information and experience right here at our door step. All these programs may be in jeopardy. Even so, there are many ways around government guidelines and expectations. I have already heard of some innovating ones.

Let me mention one more example, a totally different one. Imagine an integrated course focused on philosophy, world religions, art and cultural history, world literature and creative writing. As references students could read the likes of *Sophie's World* (a history of philosophy for teens organized around adolescents' fundamental questions about life). Some could read Joseph Campbell's writings on mythology or Carl Jung's writings on symbols; some students could even read Robert Cole's books (like, *Their Eyes Seeing the World*) or Mitch Alborn's *Tuesday's with Morrie*. When it comes to creative writings, the students could share and communicate with others all over the world. There are so many websites called *Student Art Work, Folk Tales from World Communities, Arts Ed Net*; even such outlets as website visits to art and history museums, writers, *The Pigman* project of collaborative authorship and so forth. Such an integrated study, that is concrete and grounded, immediate, beginning locally, would not only excite but also inspire and develop high quality skills in the process. The knowledge that results is first of all personal: it evokes personal response-ability. These are only examples. These are real life projects which could be drawn from any of the key dimensions and areas of life. (The only thing we would have to watch out for, of course, is which sources are corporate sponsored and distorted).

14

A Sense of Community

In closing, I would like to appeal directly to the community spirit that is evident in the towns and villages around here. There is evidence of the corporate vision of life and the distorted belief in an abstract sense of success, wealth, power, and dog-eat-dog competition all around us. Likewise, there is evidence of an each person for themselves type of attitude, wherein the economic conception of life promotes a survival of the fittest, and growth regardless of the consequences to the environment or the quality of well-being. Ultimately it is a life-distorting vision: of possession and consumption of more and more physical things and services, corporatism and consumerism.

But I also see much evidence – more than of the former – of care, of community, of responsibility for each other, of fairness and helpfulness, of neighbourliness. Communities that pay millions of dollars to the hospital, to the social agencies, to the food bank; people who volunteer and help out. I like to think that our education system could nurture that kind of life-enhancing, multidimensional vision of life in an integrated and concrete program of study. As one author puts it:

> "Another society exists within the exoskeleton of the one just described. And that society is not subject to the tunnel vision of dismal utilitarianism. It is all around us, although we analyze great economic and political questions, it is scarcely visible.
> The other society is made up of communities based in every region of the country that have formed around churches, trade unions, schools, cultural bodies, associations of various kinds, and sporting and recreational societies. The values system within these communities is vastly at odds with the global, market driven economy of the late twentieth century.

The values of this second society can be felt in any tens of thousands of decent public schools in the country (Laxer, p.188)."

In our remaining time I would like to discuss with you what we can do as parents, concerned citizens, teachers, principals and board members. To do so we need a sense of hope and empowerment, a vision of what can be and what is very near us to do. In the words of the Hebrew prophet: "Without vision a nation perishes." We all need a dream and vision of the future, to pass on to our children and grandchildren – so what is your dream and image?

Lightning Source UK Ltd.
Milton Keynes UK
UKOW030223190912

199202UK00001B/10/P

9 780957 096110